D1448990

CONTENTS

INTRODUCTION

Pizza can be found in practically every country of the world. They have become, in the last few decades, one of the mainstays of convenience and fast food eating, with pizza restaurants almost everywhere. A wide selection of fresh and frozen pizzas are also widely available from food shops and supermarkets ready for cooking at home.

From humble beginnings – when it was sold in the streets of Naples – the pizza has risen to become a sophisticated way to eat a wealth of delicious ingredients from simple cheese and tomato, cooked with fresh herbs and olive oil, to exotic shellfish, oriental vegetables and spices.

It may be imagined that making pizza at home is a difficult task, but it isn't. True, the very best results are achieved by cooking them in the traditional brick built ovens. However, few of us will have that luxury at home and excellent results can be produced from your own oven, and with very little effort. Don't be put off by making a yeast dough – you will soon learn that it is just as easy as making pastry. You will also find that there are several delicious alternative pizza bases to choose from – wholemeal, cornmeal and so on.

Pizza need not be just a snack or quick-cooked meal. They can become stylish cocktail foods, substantial pies and pastries – and even desserts – as you will see from the following pages. Included in the selection are ever-popular traditional recipes; deliciously quick and easy ideas, and pizzas designed especially for children. There is also a tempting range of pizzas to serve when entertaining, plus many international ideas.

One thing to remember. The pizza has an elegant history – being eaten by many a king or queen – so should never be considered simply a dumping ground for leftovers! It deserves better treatment than that and hopefully, with the help of *Step-by-Step Pizzas*, with more than 50 easy-to-follow recipes, you will discover a world of pizzas just waiting to be tasted!

THE HISTORY OF PIZZAS

In Naples one summer, around the late 1800's, Queen Margherita of Savoy was residing with her family in Capodimonte Park. She had heard a lot about pizza and decided to try it for herself. The local pizza maker was summoned and he served her a pizza with a newly invented topping. From then on, the tomato pulp, Mozzarella cheese and fresh basil pizza has been known as Pizza Margherita.

Until this time, pizza had been sold in the streets to people at breakfast, lunch and dinner. It was cut from a large tray that had been cooked in the baker's oven and had a simple topping made of mushrooms and anchovies.

As pizza became more popular, stalls were set up where the dough was shaped as customers ordered. Various toppings were invented including tomato, which had arrived from the New World. This soon developed into the opening of the Pizzeria, an open air place for folk to congregate, eat, drink and discuss. This has gradually become the pizza parlour we have today – which enjoys constant popularity – although the flavour of a pizza made, baked and eaten in the open air is unbeatable.

The dough base of the pizza has been baked in other countries of the Mediterranean for just as long. The French have their own Pissaladière recipe; for the Middle Eastern countries it's pitta bread and Spain uses the dough as a pastry for spicy savoury fillings. Even as far as China the same dough is steamed and served as individual stuffed snacks.

Although enjoying steady and constant popularity, it seems the pizza is now becoming a sophisticated, fashionable food with exotic toppings or turned into unusual shapes, large and small, with exciting fillings. Who knows what will happen to the pizza in years to come!

INGREDIENTS

The traditional pizzas of Italy rely on the wonderful Mediterranean ingredients that are so plentiful – sun-ripened tomatoes, thick olive oil, fresh herbs and cheese are the most well-known, but all sorts of other ingredients can be used as well. There may be some ingredients that you are not familar with.

Olive oil. Indispensable for making a genuine Italian pizza with the authentic flavour.

Olives. Both green and black are used. Olive pulp is made from crushed black olives and is obtainable in jars from Italian food shops and delicatessens.

Capers. These buds from a flowering plant have a delicious, though distinct flavour, so should be used with care.

Oregano (wild marjoram) is used on many pizzas. Use fresh wherever possible.

Thyme can be used fresh or dried.

Parsley, both flat and curly is used.

The small tender sprigs should be chosen and don't consider using the dried type for pizzas, the flavour is not nearly as good.

Basil is quite the best smelling of all the Italian herbs. Use the fresh type whenever possible.

Sweet marjoram is added to pizzas after they are cooked.

Sage should only be used fresh.

Mint should only be used fresh.

Black peppercorns should be used freshly ground as the aroma disappears very quickly, from the ready-ground type.

Nutmeg should be used freshly ground, to obtain the best flavour.

Chillies may be used in fresh form, or use whole dried or crushed type. Remember that chillies vary considerably in size and heat factor, so start with a small amount and gradually increase it.

Dried tomatoes in oil are a wonderful way to preserve tiny tomatoes. These have an unusual, distinct flavour and are available from Italian food shops and delicatessens.

Cheese. Mozzarella, Parmesan, Pecorino, Gorgonzola and Ricotta cheese are all used in traditional pizzas. (Parmesan and Pecorino are at their nicest when freshly grated from a solid piece.)

EQUIPMENT

Flat pizza tin. Metal is essential to conduct the heat and ensure that the base of the pizza is crisp.

Baking sheet. Can be used as an alternative to the flat pizza tin, however, a rim should be formed at the edge of the dough to keep the filling in place.

Rectangular tin or Swiss roll tin. For making the traditional Roman pizza or any that you wish to serve cut in squares.

Deep pan pizza tin. For the thick dough variety of pizza. A sandwich tin or pie tin may be used instead.

Pizza cutter. Makes the job of cutting a pizza far easier than using a knife.

TRADITIONAL PIZZA DOUGH

345 g (11 oz/2¾ cups) strong white flour
1 heaped teaspoon salt
15 g (½ oz/3 teaspoons) fresh (compressed) yeast; or 1 teaspoon dried active yeast and 1 teaspoon sugar; or 1 teaspoon easy blend yeast
185 ml (6 fl oz/¾ cup) hand-hot water
1 tablespoon olive oil

Put flour and salt in a large bowl.

In a small bowl, mix fresh yeast with a little water; put in a warm place until frothy. To use dried active yeast, whisk with sugar and a little water; leave until frothy. Add yeast liquid to flour with remaining water and oil. (To use easy blend yeast, mix into flour and salt before adding water and oil.) Mix to a soft dough; knead on floured surface for 10 minutes. Put in a greased bowl, cover; put in a warm place for 45 minutes or until doubled in size.

Knock back dough and knead briefly. Oil a 30 cm (12 in) pizza tin. Put dough in centre and press out to edges with knuckles. Pinch up edges to create a rim. Use as recipe instructs.

VARIATIONS

If preferred, the dough may be cooked in a 25 x 35.5 cm (10 in x 14 in) Swiss roll tin, or as 4 individual pizzas.

For Herb or Nut Pizza Dough: Knead 2 tablespoons chopped fresh herbs (or 1 tablespoon dried herbs) into the dough. If preferred, knead 30 g (1 oz/¼ cup) chopped walnuts into the dough.

For Wholemeal Pizza Dough: Use 315 g (10 oz/2¼ cups) wholemeal flour and 30 g (1 oz/¼ cup) wheat-germ. A little extra water may be required for mixing to form a soft dough. Follow the method given on page 10.

For Cornmeal Pizza Dough: Use 280 g (9 oz/2¼ cups) strong white flour and 60 g (2 oz/⅓ cup) corn-meal. Follow the method given on page 10.

POTATO PIZZA DOUGH

1 potato, about 155 g (5 oz) weight
345 g (11 oz/2¾ cups) strong white flour
1 heaped teaspoon salt
15 g (½ oz/3 teaspoons) fresh (compressed) yeast; or 1 teaspoon dried active yeast and 1 teaspoon sugar; or 1 teaspoon easy blend yeast
about 185 ml (6 fl oz/¾ cup) hand-hot water

Scrub the unpeeled potato.

Boil in the skin for 30-40 minutes. Drain and allow to cool sufficiently to remove the skin.

Put flour and salt in a bowl. In a small bowl, cream fresh yeast with a little of the water and put in a warm place until frothy. If using dried active yeast, whisk together with sugar and a little water and set aside. If using easy blend yeast, mix into flour and salt at this stage (do not add any liquid).

Sieve potato directly into flour and stir in yeast with remaining water. If using easy blend yeast, add all the hand-hot water at this stage.

Mix to a soft dough, turn onto a lightly floured surface and knead for 10 minutes until smooth. Place in a clean, lightly oiled bowl and cover with plastic wrap. Put in a warm place for about 45 minutes until dough has doubled in size.

Knock back dough and knead briefly. Oil a 30 cm (12 in) pizza tin. Place dough in the centre and press out to edges with the knuckles. Pinch up edges to create a rim. Use as recipe instructs.

Variation: Knead 2 tablespoons chopped fresh herbs or 2 table-spoons freshly grated Parmesan cheese into the dough.

DEEP PAN PIZZA DOUGH

155 g (5 oz/1 ¼ cups) strong white flour
155 g (5 oz/1 ¼ cups) plain flour
1 heaped teaspoon salt
15 g (½ oz/3 teaspoons) fresh (compressed) yeast; or 1 teaspoon dried active yeast and 1 teaspoon sugar; or 1 teaspoon easy blend yeast
185 ml (6 fl oz/¾ cup) hand-hot water
1 tablespoon olive oil

Make dough as for Traditional Pizza Dough. When dough has doubled in size, knock back and knead briefly.

Thoroughly oil a 25 cm (10 in) deep pan pizza tin or sandwich tin. Place dough in the centre and press out to edges with the knuckles.

Cover with plastic wrap and put in a warm place for about 1½ hours, until risen almost to the top of tin. Use as recipe instructs.

CRUMBLE PIZZA DOUGH

185 g (6 oz/1 ½ cups) plain flour
1 teaspoon salt
2 teaspoons caster sugar
60 ml (2 fl oz/¼ cup) vegetable oil
6 teaspoons milk

Sift flour into a large bowl. Stir in salt and sugar. Whisk oil and milk together in measuring jug and pour onto the flour.

Stir with a fork until mixture is crumbly but still moist. It will not form the usual dense dough.

Press mixture onto base and up sides of a 25 cm (10 in) deep pan pizza tin or pie tin. Use as recipe instructs.

PIZZA CARCIOFI

1 quantity Traditional Pizza Dough,
shaped and ready for topping, see pages 10
and 11

TOPPING:

2 tablespoons Tomato Topping, see page
19

60 g (2 oz/½ cup) grated Fontina cheese

280 g (9 oz) jar artichokes in oil

8 preserved tomatoes in oil

salt and pepper

parsley, to garnish

Preheat oven to 220C (425F/Gas
7). Spread the dough with Tomato
Topping. Sprinkle over the grated

Fontina cheese.

Drain artichokes, reserving the
oil. Drain the tomatoes. Slice artichokes and arrange over the
cheese. Chop tomatoes roughly and
sprinkle over the artichokes.
Season to taste with salt and
pepper. Sprinkle with 1-2 tablespoons of the reserved artichoke
oil.

Bake in the oven for 20 minutes
until dough is golden. Serve garnished with parsley.

Serves 4.

PIZZA MARINARA

1 quantity Traditional Pizza Dough,
shaped and ready for topping, see pages 10
and 11

TOPPING:

3 tablespoons olive oil

250 g (8 oz) tomatoes, skinned, see page
18

3 large cloves garlic, peeled

salt and pepper

few capers, if desired

Preheat oven to 220C (425F/Gas
7). Brush dough with 1 tablespoon
oil. Quarter tomatoes and discard
seeds. Chop roughly and drain in a
sieve. Spread over dough. Cut
garlic into thick slices and sprinkle
over tomatoes.

Season. Sprinkle with oil. Bake
in the oven for 20 minutes until
dough is crisp and golden. Sprinkle
with capers, if desired.

Serves 4.

PIZZA NAPOLITANA

1 quantity Traditional Pizza Dough, shaped and ready for topping, see pages 10 and 11

TOPPING:

3 tablespoons olive oil

500 g (1 lb) tomatoes

1 clove garlic, crushed

salt and pepper

250 g (8 oz) Mozzarella cheese

50 g (2 oz) can anchovy fillets, drained

1 tablespoon chopped fresh oregano

oregano sprigs, to garnish

Preheat oven to 220C (425F/Gas 7). Brush dough with 1 tablespoon oil. Place tomatoes in a bowl. Pour over boiling water. Leave for 1 minute. Drain, peel and roughly chop. Spread over dough. Sprinkle with garlic and season to taste with salt and pepper.

Slice cheese thin!y. Arrange over tomatoes. Chop anchovies and sprinkle over cheese. Sprinkle over oregano and remaining oil. Bake in the oven for 20 minutes until cheese has melted and dough is crisp and golden. Serve the pizza at once, garnished with a few small sprigs of oregano.

Serves 4.

PIZZA MARGHERITA

1 quantity Traditional Pizza Dough, shaped and ready for topping, see pages 10 and 11

TOMATO TOPPING:

500 g (1 lb) tomatoes, skinned, see page 18, or 440 g (14 oz) can chopped tomatoes

2 tablespoons olive oil

1 onion, finely chopped

1 clove garlic, crushed

3 teaspoons tomato purée (paste)

½ teaspoon sugar

3 teaspoons chopped fresh basil

salt and pepper

TO FINISH:

1-2 tablespoons oil

125 g (4 oz) Mozzarella cheese

6-8 fresh basil leaves

basil sprig, to garnish

Make Tomato Topping. Chop tomatoes, if using fresh. Heat oil in saucepan. Add onion and garlic and cook until soft. Stir in tomatoes, tomato purée (paste), sugar and basil and season to taste with salt and pepper. Cover pan and simmer gently for 30 minutes until thick.

Preheat oven to 220C (425F/Gas 7). Brush dough with 1 tablespoon oil. Spoon over tomato topping. Slice Mozzarella thinly. Arrange over sauce. Sprinkle with salt to taste, 2-3 basil leaves and remaining oil. Bake in the oven for 20 minutes until cheese has melted and dough is crisp and golden. Sprinkle with remaining basil leaves. Serve at once, garnished with a sprig of basil.

Serves 4.

ROMAN PIZZA

1 quantity Traditional Pizza Dough, made up to end of step 2, see pages 10 and 11

TOPPING:

3 tablespoons olive oil

2 large onions, chopped

500 g (1 lb) tomatoes, skinned, see page 18, or 440 g (14 oz) can chopped tomatoes

185 g (6 oz) can red pimento, drained

50 g (2 oz) can anchovy fillets

12 stoned black olives

pimento and olives, to garnish

Preheat oven to 220C (425F/Gas 7). Lightly grease a 25 x 35.5 cm (10 x 14 in) Swiss roll tin. Knock back risen dough and knead briefly. Place in prepared tin and press out to edges with knuckles. Pinch up edges to create a rim.

In a saucepan, heat 2 tablespoons oil. Cook onions until soft. Chop tomatoes, if fresh, add to pan and cook for 2 minutes. Spoon over dough. Slice pimento in strips and arrange over tomato. Drain anchovies, cut in half lengthwise and arrange in a lattice pattern on top. Halve olives and place in gaps. Sprinkle with remaining oil.

Bake in the oven for 20 minutes until dough is crisp and golden. Garnish with pimento and olives.

Serves 4.

FOUR SEASONS PIZZA

1 quantity Traditional Pizza Dough, made up to end of step 2, see pages 10 and 11

TOPPING:

3 tablespoons olive oil

60 g (2 oz) button mushrooms

60 g (2 oz) prosciutto (Parma ham)

6 stoned black olives

4 canned artichoke hearts, drained

60 g (2 oz) Mozzarella cheese

1 tomato, skinned, see page 18

salt and pepper

Preheat oven to 220C (425F/Gas 7). Lightly grease a baking sheet. Knock back risen dough and knead briefly. Place dough on baking sheet, press out with knuckles to a circle measuring 25 cm (10 in). Brush dough with a little oil.

Heat 2 tablespoons oil in a saucepan. Cook mushrooms for 5 minutes. Mark dough into 4 equal sections with a knife. Arrange mushrooms over one section. Cut ham in strips and chop olives; place over second section. Slice artichokes thinly. Arrange over third section. Slice cheese and tomato and arrange over fourth section. Season to taste with salt and pepper. Sprinkle with remaining oil. Bake in the oven for 20 minutes until dough is crisp and golden. Serve at once.

Serves 4.

Variation: Make this recipe as 4 individual pizzas, if preferred.

— SPICY PORK & PEPPER PIZZA —

1 quantity Traditional Pizza Dough,
shaped and ready for topping, see pages 10
and 11

TOPPING:

2 tablespoons olive oil

1 quantity Tomato Topping, see page 19

125 g (4 oz/1 cup) grated Mozzarella
cheese

3 - 4 Italian pork sausages

salt and pepper

1 yellow pepper (capsicum), seeded and
chopped

2 tablespoons freshly grated Parmesan
cheese

chopped fresh parsley, to garnish

Preheat oven to 220C (425F/Gas 7). Brush dough with 1 tablespoon oil. Spread Tomato Topping over dough. Sprinkle Mozzarella on top. With a sharp knife, cut skins from sausages and discard. Break meat into pieces, scatter over cheese. Season to taste with salt and pepper.

Sprinkle with chopped pepper (capsicum), Parmesan cheese and remaining olive oil. Bake in the oven for 20 minutes until dough is crisp. Garnish with parsley.

Serves 4.

— PROSCIUTTO & OLIVE PIZZA —

1 quantity Traditional Pizza Dough, shaped and ready for topping, see pages 10 and 11

TOPPING:

185 g (6 oz) Mozzarella cheese

4 slices prosciutto (Parma ham)

2 tablespoons olive pulp, see Note

2 tablespoons olive oil

salt and pepper

TO GARNISH:

prosciutto (Parma ham)

few olives

basil sprigs

Preheat oven to 220C (425F/Gas 7). Make the topping. Cut cheese and prosciutto (Parma ham) into cubes. Place in bowl with olive pulp. Mix together and moisten with a little oil if dry. Spread over dough. Season to taste with salt and pepper and sprinkle with remaining oil. Bake in the oven for 20 minutes until dough is crisp and golden. Garnish with curls of prosciutto (Parma ham), olives and basil sprigs.

Serves 4.

Note: Olive pulp may be bought in jars from Italian food shops.

ITALIAN SAUSAGE PIZZA

1 quantity Traditional Pizza Dough, shaped and ready for topping, see pages 10 and 11

TOPPING:

2 tablespoons olive oil

1 quantity Tomato Topping, see page 19

60 g (2 oz) mushrooms, finely sliced

3 spicy Italian sausages or 1 Luganeghe

2 tablespoons freshly grated Pecorino cheese

salt and pepper

extra grated Pecorino cheese and flat-leaf parsley, to garnish

Preheat oven to 220C (425F/Gas 7). Brush dough with 1 tablespoon oil. Spread Tomato Topping over dough and sprinkle with mushrooms. With a sharp knife, cut skins from the sausages and discard. Break meat into pieces and scatter over mushrooms. Sprinkle with grated cheese. Season to taste with salt and pepper.

Sprinkle remaining olive oil over top. Bake in the oven for 20 minutes until dough is crisp and golden. Serve garnished with extra grated Pecorino cheese and flat-leaf parsley.

Serves 4.

THREE PEPPER PIZZA

1 quantity Traditional Pizza Dough, shaped and ready for topping, see pages 10 and 11

TOPPING:

1 red pepper (capsicum)
1 yellow pepper (capsicum)
1 green pepper (capsicum)
2 tomatoes, skinned, see page 18
3 tablespoons olive oil
1 onion, finely chopped
1 clove garlic, crushed
salt and pepper
pinch of dried oregano
oregano sprigs and olives, to garnish

Make the topping. Skin peppers (capsicums): spear one at a time with a fork and hold over a gas flame for 5-10 minutes until black and blistered. Alternatively, halve and seed peppers (capsicums). Place under preheated grill until black. Peel skin off with a knife.

Chop red pepper (capsicum); quarter, seed and chop tomatoes. Put in a saucepan with 2 tablespoons oil, onion and garlic. Cook until soft. Preheat oven to 220C (425F/Gas 7). Brush dough with a little oil.

Spread pepper (capsicum) mixture over dough. Season to taste with salt and pepper. Sprinkle with oregano. Cut remaining peppers (capsicums) in strips. Arrange over pizza. Season to taste with salt and pepper. Sprinkle with remaining oil. Bake in the oven for 20 minutes until dough is crisp and golden. Garnish with oregano and olives.

Serves 4.

FOUR CHEESE PIZZA

1 quantity Traditional Pizza Dough, shaped and ready for topping, see pages 10 and 11

TOPPING:

2 tablespoons olive oil

60 g (2 oz) Mozzarella cheese

60 g (2 oz) Gorgonzola cheese

60 g (2 oz) Fontina or Gruyère cheese

60 g (2 oz/½ cup) freshly grated Parmesan cheese

salt and pepper

chopped spring onion and extra grated cheese, to garnish

Preheat oven to 220C (425F/Gas 7). Brush dough with 1 tablespoon oil. Cut the 3 cheeses into small cubes. Sprinkle over the dough. Sprinkle over Parmesan, season to taste with salt and pepper. Sprinkle over remaining oil.

Bake in the oven for 20 minutes until cheese is melted and dough is crisp and golden. Garnish with spring onion and extra cheese.

Serves 4.

CRUMPET PIZZAS

4 rashers streaky bacon, rinds removed

8 crumpets

60 g (2 oz/¼ cup) butter

2 tablespoons anchovy paste

4 tomatoes, sliced

8 slices processed Cheddar cheese

4 spring onions

stuffed olives, to garnish

Preheat grill. Grill bacon and crumpets.

Meanwhile, in a bowl, beat butter and anchovy paste together. Spread a little on each crumpet. Arrange tomato slices on top.

Cut cheese slices diagonally into 4 triangular shapes. Arrange on top of crumpets. Grill briefly to melt cheese. Slice spring onions and sprinkle on top. Cut bacon rashers in half crosswise. Roll up and spear on cocktail sticks with stuffed olives. Use to garnish crumpets and serve at once.

Serves 4.

DEVILLED MUFFINS

4 wholemeal muffins

TOPPING:

2 tablespoons vegetable oil

1 tablespoon grated fresh root ginger, if desired

375 g (12 oz) mushrooms, sliced

1 bunch spring onions, sliced

2 teaspoons Worcestershire sauce

½ teaspoon French mustard

salt and pepper

butter for spreading, if desired

spring onion tassels, to garnish

Preheat oven to 200C (400F/Gas 6). Split muffins. Toast under preheated grill on both sides.

Meanwhile make topping. Heat oil in a large saucepan. Add ginger, if desired, and fry for 10-15 seconds, stirring.

Add mushrooms; cook stirring for 1 minute. Add spring onions and continue to cook for 10 seconds. Add Worcestershire sauce and mustard and season to taste with salt and pepper. Butter muffins, if desired. Spoon mushroom mixture on top of muffins and bake in the oven for 2-3 minutes. Serve at once, garnished with spring onion tassels.

Serves 4.

– AUBERGINE & TOMATO PIZZA –

1 quantity Traditional Pizza Dough, shaped and ready for topping, see pages 10 and 11

AUBERGINE TOPPING:

500 g (1 lb) aubergines (eggplants)

1 clove garlic, crushed

3 tablespoons lemon juice

3 tablespoons chopped fresh parsley

2 spring onions, chopped

salt and pepper

TO FINISH:

500 g (1 lb) tomatoes, sliced

1 tablespoon olive oil

2 tablespoons chopped fresh parsley

2 tablespoons freshly grated Parmesan cheese

parsley sprigs, to garnish

First make Aubergine Topping. Preheat oven to 180C (350F/Gas 4). Put aubergines (eggplants) on a baking sheet and bake in the oven for 30 minutes until soft. Cool.

Halve and scoop out soft centres into a bowl. Add garlic, lemon juice, parsley and spring onions. Season to taste with salt and pepper.

Increase oven temperature to 220C (425F/Gas 7). Spread aubergine (eggplant) purée over dough. Arrange sliced tomatoes on top, brush with oil and season to taste with salt and pepper. Sprinkle with chopped parsley and Parmesan cheese. Bake in the oven for 20 minutes. Serve garnished with parsley.

Serves 4.

Note: The aubergine purée may be made in advance and refrigerated for 3-4 days. It is also delicious served as a dip with hot toast or pitta bread.

FRENCH BREAD PIZZA

1 medium French stick
4 tablespoons olive oil
440 g (14 oz) can tomatoes
salt and pepper
220 g (7 oz) can tuna fish in oil, drained
6-8 pimento-stuffed olives
60 g (2 oz/½ cup) grated Edam cheese
3 spring onions, chopped
TO SERVE:
green salad

Preheat oven to 180C (350F/Gas 4). Cut a slice from the top of French stick along whole length. Scoop out most of the soft crumb from base portion (this and the lid will not be required but can be used for breadcrumbs).

Brush inside of loaf with half the olive oil. Drain tomatoes and reserve juice. Brush inside of loaf with juice. Place loaf on a baking sheet and bake in the oven for 10 minutes.

Chop tomatoes and arrange half inside the loaf. Season to taste with salt and pepper. Flake tuna fish and spoon over tomatoes. Season again. Top with remaining tomatoes and season once again.

Halve olives and arrange on top. Sprinkle with grated cheese. Return to oven and bake for a further 15 minutes. Sprinkle with chopped spring onions and serve at once with salad.

Serves 2.

TAPENADE & PEPPER PIZZA

1 quantity Deep Pan Pizza Dough, shaped and ready for topping, see page 14
TAPENADE TOPPING:
155 g (5 oz) stoned green olives
60 g (2 oz) can anchovy fillets
60 g (2 oz) canned tuna fish in oil, drained
30 g (1 oz) capers
1 clove garlic
1 teaspoon Dijon mustard
a little olive oil
salt and pepper
a little lemon juice
TO FINISH:
1 green pepper (capsicum), skinned, see page 26
1 yellow pepper (capsicum), skinned
mint sprigs and a few capers, to garnish

Preheat oven to 220C (425F/Gas 7). Make the topping. In a blender or food processor, put the olives, anchovy fillets and oil, tuna fish, capers, garlic and mustard. Blend to a rough-textured purée. Add a little extra oil if necessary. Season with salt and pepper and lemon juice.

Cut skinned peppers (capsicums) into strips and then into diamond shapes. Spread tapenade over dough. Arrange peppers attractively on top. Trickle a little more oil over and season with pepper. Bake in the oven for 20 minutes until dough is golden and well risen. Serve garnished with mint sprigs and capers.

Serves 4.

— PESTO & MUSHROOM PIZZA —

1 quantity Deep Pan Pizza Dough, shaped and ready for topping, see page 14

PESTO TOPPING:

1 large bunch fresh basil leaves

3 cloves garlic, peeled

60 g (2 oz/⅓ cup) pine nuts

3 tablespoons freshly grated Parmesan cheese

salt and pepper

155 ml (5 fl oz/⅔ cup) olive oil

a little boiling water

TO FINISH:

185 g (6 oz) button mushrooms, sliced

a little olive oil

90 g (3 oz/⅔ cup) grated Mozzarella cheese

90 g (3 oz/⅔ cup) freshly grated Parmesan cheese

basil sprigs and pine nuts, to garnish

Preheat oven to 220C (425F/Gas 7). Make topping. In a blender or food processor, put basil leaves, garlic, pine nuts and Parmesan cheese and season to taste with salt and pepper. Switch on machine and pour in oil in a gentle stream until absorbed. Blend until smooth, adding a little boiling water if necessary, to achieve a spreading consistency.

Spread topping over dough. Arrange mushrooms on top; brush with olive oil. Sprinkle with Mozzarella cheese and Parmesan cheese. Bake in the oven for 20 minutes until dough is well risen and golden. Serve garnished with basil and pine nuts.

Serves 4.

Note: Pesto can be made in advance and stored in a screw-topped jar in the refrigerator for up to 6 days. Ready-made pesto may be bought from delicatessen counters in supermarkets and from specialist food shops.

CHEESY SEAFOOD PIZZA

1 quantity Traditional Pizza Dough, shaped and ready for topping, see pages 10 and 11

TOPPING:

1 quantity Cheese Topping, see page 35

220 g (7 oz) can tuna fish in brine

185 g (6 oz) peeled prawns, thawed if frozen

¼ teaspoon paprika

salt and pepper

lemon twists, coriander sprigs and peeled prawns, to garnish, if desired

Preheat oven to 220C (425F/Gas 7). Spread the Cheese Topping over the pizza dough.

Drain tuna fish, put in a bowl and flake roughly with a fork. Mix in prawns and paprika and season to taste with salt and pepper. Spread mixture evenly over the Cheese Topping.

Bake in the oven for 20 minutes until the dough is crisp and golden. Serve the pizza at once, garnished with lemon twists, sprigs of coriander and peeled prawns, if desired.

Serves 4.

CREAMY SALMON PIZZA

1 quantity Wholemeal Pizza Dough,
shaped and ready for topping, see pages 10
and 11

1 tablespoon olive oil

TOPPING:

439 g (15½ oz) can red salmon

1 courgette (zucchini), finely chopped

3 tablespoons double (thick) cream

salt and pepper

1 teaspoon grated lemon peel

1 tablespoon chopped fresh dill

30 g (1 oz/¼ cup) grated Parmesan
cheese

lemon peel and dill sprigs, to garnish

Preheat oven to 220C (425F/Gas
7). Make the topping. Drain
salmon and remove bones. Put in a
bowl and flake with a fork. Stir in
courgette (zucchini), cream, salt
and pepper, lemon peel and dill.

Brush dough with olive oil.
Spoon the salmon mixture on top.
Sprinkle with the Parmesan cheese.
Bake in the oven for 20 minutes
until the dough is golden. Serve
garnished with lemon and dill.

Serves 4.

CHEESE & ONION PIZZAS

8 small pitta breads
CHEESE TOPPING:
30 g (1 oz/6 teaspoons) butter or margarine
15 g (½ oz/6 teaspoons) plain flour
250 g (8 oz/2 cups) grated Cheddar cheese
75 ml (2½ fl oz/⅓ cup) milk
1 egg yolk
pinch of dry mustard
pinch of cayenne pepper
TO FINISH:
3 spring onions, chopped
2 eggs, hard-boiled and chopped
hard-boiled egg and chives, to garnish

Preheat oven to 220C (425F/Gas 7). Make the topping. In a saucepan, melt butter or magarine. Add flour and cook, stirring, until smooth. Stir in half the grated cheese, then half the milk. Repeat with remaining cheese and milk. Beat in egg yolk. Stir in mustard and cayenne pepper and mix well.

Place pitta breads on a greased baking sheet. Spread topping over them. Bake in the oven for 10 minutes. In a bowl, mix chopped spring onions and hard-boiled eggs together. Sprinkle the mixture over the pizzas and cook for a further 2 minutes. Serve at once, garnished with slices of hard-boiled egg and chives.

Serves 4.

FRITTATA PIZZA

1 quantity Traditional Pizza Dough, made up to end of step 2, see pages 10 and 11
TOPPING:
2 tablespoons olive oil
1 onion, thinly sliced
3 new potatoes, cooked and sliced
8 slices pepper salami, rind removed
1 small green pepper (capsicum), sliced
8 stoned black olives, halved
60 g (2 oz/⅓ cup) full fat soft cheese, cubed
1 tablespoon chopped fresh parsley
4 cherry tomatoes, halved
6 eggs
salt and pepper
watercress, to garnish

Preheat oven to 220C (425F/Gas 7). Grease a 25 cm (10 in) deep pan pizza tin or sandwich tin. Knock back risen dough and knead briefly, then press dough into tin.

Brush dough with a little of the oil. Arrange sliced onion over the top. Sprinkle with remaining oil. Bake in the oven for 10 minutes.

Remove pizza from oven. Arrange sliced potatoes, salami, pepper (capsicum), olives and cheese over the surface. Add parsley and tomatoes. In a bowl, beat together eggs and season to taste with salt and pepper. Pour over pizza and bake for 10-15 minutes until topping is puffed and golden. Serve garnished with watercress.

Serves 4.

GRAVLAX MUFFINS

6 muffins

TOPPING:

125 g (4 oz/½ cup) butter, softened

1 teaspoon honey

2 teaspoons French mustard

2 teaspoons lemon juice

1 tablespoon chopped fresh dill

salt and pepper

350 g (12 oz) gravlax or smoked salmon

thick sour cream and dill sprigs,
to garnish

Preheat oven to 220C (425F/Gas 7). Halve the muffins and place them on a baking sheet. Bake in the oven for 5 minutes.

Meanwhile, in a bowl beat the butter with the honey, French mustard, lemon juice and chopped fresh dill. Season to taste with salt and pepper.

Spread the butter mixture over the muffins and top with the gravlax or smoked salmon, dividing it equally between them. Bake in the oven for 5 minutes, then serve at once, garnished with thick sour cream and sprigs of dill.

Serves 6.

AVOCADO & CRAB BITES

1 quantity Traditional Pizza Dough, made up to end of step 2, see pages 10 and 11
TOPPING:
2 ripe avocados
1 tablespoon lemon juice
30 g (1 oz/6 teaspoons) butter
30 g (1 oz/¼ cup) plain flour
315 ml (10 fl oz/1¼ cups) milk
salt and pepper
¼ teaspoon cayenne pepper
375 g (12 oz) crabmeat, thawed if frozen and drained
60 g (2 oz/½ cup) grated Gruyère cheese
avocado slices and tomato, to garnish

Preheat oven to 220C (425F/Gas 7). Knock back risen dough and knead briefly. Roll out dough and use to line a Swiss roll tin.

Make topping. Halve avocados, remove stones. Scoop out flesh and chop roughly. Place in a bowl with lemon juice and stir lightly to coat. Set aside.

Melt butter in a saucepan. Stir in flour and cook for 2 minutes. Stir in milk, bring to the boil and simmer for 2 minutes. Season to taste with salt and pepper and cayenne.

Remove pan from heat. Stir in crab, cheese and avocado. Spread over the dough, then bake in the oven for 20 minutes until dough is golden. Cool slightly before cutting into fingers or squares. Serve garnished with avocado and tomato.

Serves 6-8.

CORONATION CHICKEN PIZZA

1 quantity Traditional Pizza Dough, shaped and ready for topping, see pages 10 and 11

TOPPING:
375 g (12 oz) cooked chicken meat, cubed
60 g (2 oz/¹/₃ cup) roasted cashew nuts
1 small leek, finely shredded
3 tablespoons mayonnaise
3 tablespoons Greek natural yogurt
1 teaspoon curry powder
1 tablespoon apricot jam
1 tablespoon mango chutney, chopped
2 tablespoons chopped fresh coriander
salt and pepper
lemon juice, to taste
coriander, to garnish

Preheat oven to 220C (425F/Gas 7). Make the topping. In a bowl, mix chicken, cashew nuts and leek. In a second bowl, mix mayonnaise, yogurt, curry powder, jam, chutney and coriander. Season to taste with salt and pepper and lemon juice. Mix sauce with the chicken mixture. Spoon chicken mixture on top of the dough. Bake in the oven for 20 minutes until the dough is golden. Serve at once, garnished with coriander.

Serves 4.

Variation: Substitute other cooked and cubed meat, such as ham, pork, or lamb for the chicken and use roasted almonds, roughly chopped, instead of the cashew nuts.

TARRAGON TROUT PARCEL

1 quantity Potato Pizza Dough, made up to end of step 5, see pages 12 and 13

FILLING:

500 g (1 lb) pink trout fillets, skinned

625 ml (20 fl oz/2½ cups) white wine

few parsley and tarragon sprigs

salt and pepper

60 g (2 oz/¼ cup) butter

60 g (2 oz/½ cup) plain flour

2 tablespoons single (light) cream

125 g (4 oz) peeled prawns, thawed if frozen

60 g (2 oz) mushrooms, sliced

beaten egg, to glaze

4 teaspoons sesame seeds

prawns, lemon and tarragon sprigs, to garnish

Make the filling. Put fish and wine in a saucepan with parsley and tarragon sprigs and season with a little salt and pepper. Bring to the boil, cover and remove from the heat. Leave to cool. Drain and reserve liquor. Flake fish.

Melt butter in a saucepan. Add flour and cook, stirring. Add reserved liquid to make a smooth sauce. Remove from heat, stir in fish, cream, prawns and mushrooms. Check seasoning. Cool.

Preheat oven to 220C (425F/Gas 7). Grease a baking sheet. Knock back risen dough and knead briefly. Roll out dough on a lightly floured surface to a square measuring 30 cm (12 in). Place on baking sheet. Spoon filling in centre. Brush edges with beaten egg. Fold corners of dough to centre; pinch seams to seal. Brush with beaten egg and sprinkle with sesame seeds. Bake for 25-30 minutes. Serve garnished with prawns, lemon and tarragon.

Serves 4-6.

HAM & TOMATO BITES

1 quantity Traditional Pizza Dough, made to end of step 2, see pages 10 and 11

TOPPING:

1 quantity Tomato Topping, see page 19
12-14 slices coppa, or Parma, smoked ham
185 g (6 oz) Mozzarella cheese, sliced
olives, anchovies and thyme sprigs, to garnish

Preheat oven to 220C (425F/Gas 7). Grease several baking sheets. Roll out dough very thinly and cut out 12-14 circles with a 4-5 cm (1½-2 in) cutter.

Spread dough with Tomato Topping. Top each circle with a slice of coppa, or Parma, ham and a slice of Mozzarella. Bake in the oven for 10-15 minutes until the dough is cooked and the cheese has melted. Serve at once, garnished with olives, anchovies and thyme.

Serves 6-8.

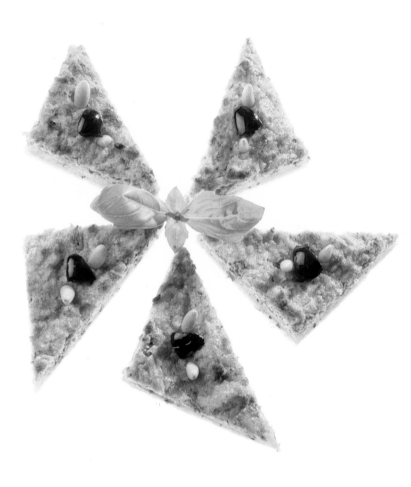

PESTO PIZZELLE

1 quantity Traditional Pizza Dough, made to end of step 2, see pages 10 and 11

TOPPING:

185 g (6 oz) ricotta cheese

3 tablespoons Pesto Topping, see page 32

1 egg, beaten

basil sprigs, black olives and pine nuts, to garnish

Preheat oven to 220C (425F/Gas 7). Knock back risen dough and knead briefly. Roll out dough and use to line a Swiss roll tin.

Make the topping. Beat together ricotta cheese and sufficient Pesto Topping and egg to make a smooth, firm mixture.

Spread over the dough, then bake in the oven for 20 minutes until the dough is golden. Cool slightly, then cut into squares or triangles. Garnish with basil, olives and pine nuts. Serve as a cocktail snack.

Serves 10-20.

— ASPARAGUS HAM SQUARES —

1 quantity Traditional Pizza Dough, made
up to end of step 2, see pages 10 and 11

1 tablespoon vegetable oil

TOPPING:

185 g (6 oz) sliced ham

185 g (6 oz) curd cheese

2 tablespoons single (light) cream or milk

250 g (8 oz) asparagus spears, cooked

salt and pepper

freshly grated Parmesan cheese

Preheat oven to 220 C (425F/Gas
7). Grease a 25 x 35.5 cm (10 x 14
in) Swiss roll tin. Knock back risen
dough and knead briefly. Roll out
dough on a lightly floured surface
and use to line base and sides of tin.
Prick base with a fork. Brush with
oil. Bake in the oven for 15 minutes
until crisp and golden.

Meanwhile, finely chop 125 g

(4 oz) ham. Put in a bowl with the
cheese and cream or milk. Cut tips
from asparagus and reserve. Chop
stalks and stir into cheese mixture.

Remove pizza from oven and
allow to cool slightly. Spread cheese
mixture over dough. Slice remaining ham in strips and arrange in a
lattice pattern over dough. Dot
asparagus tips on surface, season to
taste with salt and pepper and
sprinkle with Parmesan cheese.
Return to oven and cook for a
further 2 minutes. Slide pizza from
tin onto a chopping board. With a
sharp knife cut off crusts and discard. Cut pizza into small squares or
fingers (or other shapes, if preferred)
and serve as a cocktail snack.

Serves 8-10.

RATATOUILLE & PRAWN PIZZA

1 quantity Wholemeal Pizza Dough, shaped and ready for topping, see pages 10 and 11

1 tablespoon vegetable oil

TOPPING:

2 tablespoons vegetable oil

1 large onion, chopped

2 cloves garlic, crushed

3 small courgettes (zucchini), halved

1 small red pepper (capsicum), seeded

1 small green pepper (capsicum), seeded

1 small yellow pepper (capsicum), seeded

250 g (8 oz) aubergine (eggplant), cubed

440 g (14 oz) can chopped tomatoes

2 tablespoons tomato purée (paste)

salt and pepper

125 g (4 oz) peeled prawns, thawed if frozen

chopped parsley, to garnish

Make the topping. Heat oil in a large saucepan. Add onion and garlic. Cook for 3 minutes, stirring and taking care not to let garlic burn.

Cut courgettes (zucchini) and peppers (capsicums) into 1 cm (½ in) pieces. Add to pan with aubergine (eggplant). Add tomatoes, tomato purée (paste) and season to taste with salt and pepper. Stir well and cook for 15 minutes until vegetables are cooked and the sauce thickened.

Preheat oven to 220 C (425F/Gas 7). Prick dough with a fork and brush with oil. Bake in the oven for 15 minutes. Stir prawns into vegetables and spoon on top of dough. Bake for a further 5 minutes. Serve at once sprinkled with chopped parsley.

Serves 4.

MIXED SEAFOOD PIZZA

1 quantity Traditional Pizza Dough, shaped and ready for topping, see pages 10 and 11
TOPPING:
250 g (8 oz) mussels in the shell
2 tablespoons olive oil
2 cloves garlic, crushed
125 g (4 oz) squid, cleaned
440 g (14 oz) can chopped tomatoes
salt and pepper
125 g (4 oz) raw Mediterranean (king) prawns, thawed if frozen
250 g (8 oz) clean shelled clams or 144 g (14 oz) canned clams in brine, drained
2 tablespoons chopped fresh parsley
flat-leaf parsley and lemon, to garnish

Make topping. Scrub mussels and remove beards. Place in a large saucepan with 2 tablespoons water. Cover and cook over moderate heat, shaking pan, until all the shells are open.

Strain pan juices and reserve. In a saucepan, heat 1 tablespoon oil and garlic. Slice squid and add to pan. Cook for 5 minutes, stirring. Remove with a slotted spoon and reserve. Discard garlic. Add tomatoes, reserved mussel juice and season to taste with salt and pepper. Cook gently for 30 minutes.

Preheat oven to 220C (425F/Gas 7). Brush dough with remaining oil; prick with a fork. Bake in the oven for 15-20 minutes until golden. Peel prawns; add to sauce with the clams. Cook for 10 minutes. Stir in squid and mussels. Remove pizza from oven. Spoon over fish and sauce, sprinkle with chopped parsley and return to oven for 10 minutes. Garnish with parsley and lemon and serve at once.

Serves 4.

PIZZA CANAPÉS

1 quantity Cornmeal Pizza Dough, made up to end of step 2, see pages 10 and 11

TOPPING:

1 quantity Cheese Topping, see page 35
a selection of the following: anchovy fillets, stuffed and plain; olives; capers; lumpfish roe; cooked prawns; smoked salmon; crispy bacon; smoked quails' eggs; sprigs of fresh herbs

Preheat oven to 220C (425F/Gas 7). Grease several baking sheets. Knock back risen dough and knead briefly. Roll out dough very thinly and cut out 10-12 small circles with a 4-5 cm (1½-2 in) cutter (or cut into fingers, if preferred). Spread with a little Cheese Topping and arrange on baking sheets. Bake in the oven for 15-20 minutes until golden. Top with any selection of toppings and serve at once.

Serves 10-12.

HAM & CHEESE PARTY PIZZAS

1 quantity Cornmeal Pizza Dough, made up to end of step 2, see pages 10 and 11
1 tablespoon olive oil

TOPPING:

1 quantity Tomato Topping, see page 19
6 slices prosciutto (Parma ham)
10-12 stoned black or green olives
freshly grated Parmesan cheese and thyme sprigs, to garnish

Preheat oven to 220C (425F/Gas 7). Grease several baking sheets. Knock back risen dough and knead briefly. Roll out dough and cut as for Pizza Canapés, see page 50. Brush with oil and bake in the oven for 15-20 minutes until golden.

Spread each circle with a little Tomato Topping. Cut prosciutto into 10-12 pieces. Fold each piece into a cornet shape and place on top of a circle. Place an olive in each cone and sprinkle with Parmesan cheese. Return to oven for 3 minutes to soften cheese. Serve at once, garnished with cheese and thyme.

Serves 10-12.

GORGONZOLA & NUT SHAPES

1 quantity Traditional Pizza Dough, made up to end of step 2, see pages 10 and 11

TOPPING:

185 g (6 oz) Gorgonzola cheese

185 g (6 oz) Mozzarella cheese

10 walnut halves

3 tablespoons walnut oil

cucumber, to garnish

Preheat oven to 220C (425F/Gas 7). Grease a 25 x 35.5 cm (10 x 14 in) Swiss roll tin. Knock back risen dough and knead briefly. Roll out dough on a lightly floured surface and use to line base and sides of tin.

Cut Gorgonzola and Mozzarella cheeses into small cubes. Roughly chop walnuts. Brush surface of dough with a little walnut oil. Sprinkle cheese over and top with walnuts. Sprinkle with remaining oil.

Bake in the oven for 20 minutes until dough is crisp and golden. Slide from tin onto a chopping board. Cut crusts off with a sharp knife and discard. Cut pizza into small squares and fingers. Garnish with cucumber and serve at once as a cocktail snack.

Serves 8-10.

MOZZOLIVE BITES

1 quantity Cornmeal Pizza Dough, made up to end of step 2, see pages 10 and 11
TOPPING:
4 tablespoons olive oil
185 g (6 oz) Mozzarella cheese
170 g (5½ oz) jar olive paste
salt and pepper
sage leaves and pimento, to garnish

Preheat oven to 220C (425F/Gas 7). Grease several baking sheets. Knock back risen dough and knead briefly. Roll out dough and cut as for Pizza Canapés, see page 50. Brush with 1 tablespoon oil and bake in the oven for 15-20 minutes until golden.

Cut Mozzarella into tiny pieces and place in a bowl. Stir in the olive paste. Season to taste with salt and pepper. Spoon a little of the mixture onto each circle, dividing it equally between them.

Sprinkle with a little oil. Bake for a further 3-4 minutes until cheese melts. Garnish with sage leaves and pimento. Serve at once as a cocktail snack.

Serves 10-12.

ARTICHOKE & EMMENTAL PIZZA

1 quantity Traditional Pizza Dough,
shaped and ready for topping, see pages 10
and 11

TOPPING:

3 tablespoons olive oil

440 g (14 oz) can artichoke hearts

salt and pepper

250 g (8 oz/2 cups) grated Emmental
cheese

marjoram leaves and sliced pimento, to
garnish

Preheat oven to 220C (425F/Gas 7). Brush the pizza dough with 1 tablespoon of the olive oil.

Drain artichokes and slice thinly. Arrange artichoke slices over dough. Sprinkle with remaining oil; season to taste with salt and pepper. Sprinkle the grated Emmental cheese over the top.

Bake in the oven for 20 minutes until dough is crisp and golden and cheese has melted. Serve at once, garnished with marjoram leaves and sliced pimento.

Serves 4.

MIDDLE EASTERN PIZZA

1 quantity Wholemeal Pizza Dough, shaped and ready for topping, see pages 10 and 11

TOPPING:

500 g (1 lb) minced beef

1 tablespoon olive oil

1 onion, finely chopped

1 clove garlic, crushed

1 teaspoon ground allspice

1 teaspoon ground cumin

salt and pepper

2 tablespoons tomato purée (paste)

155 ml (5 fl oz/⅔ cup) stock

60 g (2 oz/½ cup) dried apricots, chopped finely

2 tablespoons chopped fresh coriander

juice of 1 lemon or lime

30 g (1 oz/2 tablespoons) pine nuts

1 tablespoon sesame seeds

lime slices and coriander sprigs, to garnish

TO SERVE:

natural yogurt

Preheat oven to 190C (375F/Gas 5). In a saucepan, cook minced beef with the olive oil, onion and garlic until brown, stirring occasionally to prevent lumps of meat forming.

Stir in the allspice, cumin, salt and pepper to taste, tomato purée (paste) and stock. Cover; cook for 10 minutes, stirring occasionally.

Stir the chopped dried apricots, chopped coriander, lemon or lime juice and pine nuts into the meat mixture. Spoon the mixture over the dough and sprinkle sesame seeds over the top. Bake in the oven for 20 minutes until the dough is crisp and golden.

Garnish with lime slices and sprigs of coriander and serve at once with natural yogurt.

Serves 4-6.

PISSALADIÈRE

1 quantity Traditional Pizza Dough, shaped and ready for topping, see pages 10 and 11

TOPPING:

440 g (14 oz) can crushed tomatoes

1 onion, chopped

1 clove garlic, crushed

2 tablespoons olive oil

1 tablespoon chopped fresh parsley

2 teaspoons chopped fresh thyme or 1 teaspoon dried thyme

1 tablespoon tomato purée (paste)

1 egg

60 g (2 oz/½ cup) grated Gruyère cheese

salt and pepper

90 g (3 oz) can anchovy fillets

black olives

thyme sprigs and Gruyère cheese, to garnish, if desired

Make the topping. In a saucepan, heat tomatoes, onion, garlic, 1 tablespoon oil, parsley, thyme and tomato purée (paste) together. Bring to the boil, reduce heat; simmer 30 minutes. Cool slightly.

Preheat oven to 200C (400F/Gas 6). Brush dough with remaining oil.

Beat egg and stir into tomato mixture with grated cheese. Spread over dough. Season to taste with salt and pepper. Drain and cut anchovy fillets in thin strips. Arrange in a lattice over pizza. Add olives and bake in the oven for 20 minutes until dough is crisp and golden. Serve garnished with thyme and Gruyère cheese, if desired.

Serves 4.

SAUSAGE & APPLE PIZZA

1 quantity Wholemeal Pizza Dough, made up to end of step 2, see pages 10 and 11

2 tablespoons vegetable oil

TOPPING:

500 g (1 lb) pork sausages with herbs

1 cooking apple, cored

3 tablespoons apple juice or cider

2 tablespoons mild mustard

salt and pepper

1 red eating apple

1 green eating apple

a little lemon juice

TO SERVE:

small packet potato crisps

Preheat oven to 200C (400F/Gas 6). Lightly grease a 25 x 35.5 cm (10 x 14 in) Swiss roll tin. Knock back risen dough and knead briefly. Place in tin and press over base and up sides with the knuckles. Brush with 1 tablespoon oil.

Remove skin from the sausages by splitting with a sharp knife. Put sausagemeat in a bowl. Grate cooking apple, stir into sausagemeat with apple juice or cider and mustard and season to taste with salt and pepper. Spread the mixture evenly over pizza dough.

Core red and green eating apples. Slice thinly and brush cut surfaces with lemon juice. Arrange over sausagemeat and brush with remaining 1 tablespoon oil. Bake in the oven for 20 minutes until dough is crisp and golden. Crush potato crisps roughly and sprinkle over top of pizza.

Serves 6.

POTATO PIZZA SQUARES

1 quantity Wholemeal Pizza Dough, made up to end of step 2, see pages 10 and 11

1 tablespoon vegetable oil

TOPPING:

8 small potatoes, peeled

salt

1 quantity Tomato Topping, see page 19

60 g (2 oz/½ cup) grated Cheddar cheese

cucumber slices and sliced spring onion, to garnish

Cook potatoes for topping in salted boiling water for 10-15 minutes. Drain, cool slightly; slice thinly.

Meanwhile, preheat oven to 220C (425F/Gas 7). Grease a Swiss roll tin. Knock back risen dough and knead briefly. Roll out and use to line the Swiss roll tin. Brush with oil.

Spread Tomato Topping over dough. Arrange potato slices on top and sprinkle with grated cheese. Bake in the oven for 20 minutes. Serve cut into squares, garnished with cucumber and spring onion.

Serves 6-8.

PIZZA FACES

freshly-baked or bought, ready-made individual pizza bases

TOPPING:

4 tablespoons tomato ketchup (sauce) or chutney

6-8 processed Cheddar cheese slices

alfalfa sprouts or grated carrot

olive slices

pepper (capsicum) strips

Preheat oven to 200C (400F/Gas 6). Spread pizza bases with ketchup or chutney. Arrange cheese over top to represent skin. Place on a baking sheet and bake in the oven for 10-15 minutes until melted.

Give each child the prepared ingredients to make their own pizza face, using alfalfa sprouts or carrot as hair, olive slices for eyes and pepper (capsicum) strips for mouth.

Serves 2.

Variations: Many other ingredients can be used in place of those listed and children will enjoy making different expressions on the faces.

BLT PIZZA

1 quantity Traditional Pizza Dough,
shaped and ready for topping, see pages 10
and 11

FILLING:

8 streaky bacon rashers, rinds removed

½ small iceberg lettuce

4 tomatoes, roughly chopped

4-6 tablespoons mayonnaise

salt and pepper

shredded lettuce, to garnish

Preheat oven to 200C (400F/Gas
6). Grill bacon until cooked. Drain

on absorbent kitchen paper, then
with kitchen scissors, cut into
pieces. Very finely shred the lettuce.
In a bowl, mix bacon, tomatoes,
lettuce and mayonnaise and season
to taste with salt and pepper.

Spread the mixture over the
dough. Bake in the oven for 20
minutes until the dough is crisp and
golden. Serve at once, garnished
with shredded lettuce.

Serves 4.

GAMMON & PINEAPPLE PIZZA

8 crumpets

TOPPING:

1 quantity Cheese Topping, see page 35

185 g (6 oz) cooked gammon or shoulder
ham, minced or finely chopped

salt and pepper

8 canned pineapple rings

chopped parsley, tomato wedges and
pineapple, to garnish

Preheat oven to 220C (425F/Gas 7).
Spread Cheese Topping evenly over
crumpets. Pile ham on top. Season
with salt and pepper.

Place a pineapple ring on each
crumpet. Bake in the oven for 10-
15 minutes. Serve garnished with
parsley and a cocktail stick speared
with pineapple and tomato.

Serves 8.

BREAKFAST PIZZA

1 quantity Traditional Pizza Dough, shaped and ready for topping, see pages 10 and 11

3 tablespoons vegetable oil

TOPPING:

440 g (14 oz) can chopped tomatoes

salt and pepper

8 streaky bacon rashers, rinds removed

4 eggs

Preheat oven to 220C (425F/Gas 7). Brush dough with 1 tablespoon oil.

Spoon chopped tomatoes over dough. Season to taste with salt and pepper. Arrange bacon over the tomatoes, leaving 4 gaps, equally spaced. Sprinkle with remaining oil and bake in the oven for 15 minutes.

Remove from oven. Break an egg into each of the 4 gaps. Return pizza to oven for about 10 minutes until the whites are set but the yolks still liquid. Serve at once.

Serves 4.

MINCE & PICKLE PIZZA

1 quantity Potato Pizza Dough, shaped and ready for topping, see pages 12 and 13

TOPPING:

250 g (8 oz) ground beef

salt and pepper

2 tablespoons tomato purée (paste)

2 tablespoons Worcestershire sauce

3 tablespoons vegetable oil

4 tablespoons sweet pickle

125 g (4 oz) mushrooms, sliced

1 green pepper (capsicum), sliced

1 small onion, sliced

watercress, chives and red pepper (capsicum), to garnish

Make the topping. In a saucepan, cook the beef until browned. Season to taste with salt and pepper. Add tomato purée (paste) and Worcestershire sauce. Cook for 15 minutes, stirring the mixture occasionally.

Preheat oven to 220C (425F/Gas 7). Brush dough with 1 tablespoon oil. Spread pickle over the dough. Arrange mushrooms on top. Spoon meat mixture on top. Arrange rings of pepper (capsicum) and onion over and brush with remaining oil. Bake in the oven for 20 minutes until dough is crisp and golden. Serve garnished with watercress bunches tied with chives and red pepper (capsicum).

Serves 4.

— SARDINE & TOMATO PIZZA —

1 quantity Traditional Pizza Dough,
shaped and ready for topping, see pages 10
and 11

TOPPING:

4 tablespoons tomato ketchup (sauce)

125 g (4 oz) can sardines in oil, drained

2 tomatoes, sliced

4 processed cheese slices

mustard and cress, to garnish

Preheat oven to 220C (425F/Gas
7). Spread tomato ketchup (sauce)
over the dough. Split sardines hori-
zontally and arrange around the
edge. Make a circle of overlapping
tomatoes in the centre.

Cut cheese in strips and arrange
in a lattice over the tomatoes. Bake
in the oven for 20 minutes until the
dough is golden. Serve at once,
garnished with mustard and cress.

Serves 6.

BOLOGNESE PIZZA

1 quantity Potato Pizza Dough, with
Parmesan cheese, shaped and ready for
topping, see pages 12 and 13

TOPPING:

2 tablespoons vegetable oil

60 g (2 oz) rashers streaky bacon,
chopped

1 onion, finely chopped

1 carrot, finely chopped

1 stick celery, finely chopped

1 clove garlic, crushed

250 g (8 oz) ground beef

1 tablespoon tomato purée (paste)

pinch of mixed herbs

125 ml (4 fl oz/½ cup) beef stock

salt and pepper

TO SERVE:

freshly grated Parmesan cheese

tomato and marjoram sprigs, to garnish

Make the topping. In a saucepan, heat oil and cook the bacon for 2 minutes. Add onion, carrot, celery and garlic. Cook, stirring, until soft. Add ground beef and cook, stirring until brown.

Stir in tomato purée (paste), herbs and stock and season to taste with salt and pepper. Cover and cook gently for 30 minutes.

Preheat oven to 220C (425F/Gas 7). Spoon sauce on top of dough and spread over. Bake in the oven for 20 minutes until dough is crisp and golden. Serve sprinkled with Parmesan cheese and garnished with tomato and marjoram.

Serves 6.

TUNA & ONION PIZZA

1 quantity Deep Pan Pizza Dough, shaped
and ready for topping, see page 14

TOPPING:

2 tablespoons vegetable oil

440 g (14 oz) can chopped tomatoes

1 bunch spring onions, chopped

220 g (7 oz) can tuna fish, drained

salt and pepper

Preheat oven to 220C (425F/Gas
7). Brush dough with 1 tablespoon
oil. Bake in the oven for 20 minutes
until golden and well risen.

Make the topping. In a saucepan, heat the tomatoes and remaining oil. Add half the spring onions
to pan and cook for 10 minutes.
Flake tuna fish roughly, stir into
tomato mixture. Season to taste
with salt and pepper.

Spoon onto dough and bake in
the oven for 3-5 minutes. Shred
remaining chopped spring onions
and sprinkle over pizza to serve.

Serves 6.

MUSHROOM & CHEESE PIZZA

1 quantity Wholemeal Pizza Dough, shaped and ready for topping, see pages 10 and 11

TOPPING:

1-2 tablespoons French mustard or 30 g (1 oz/6 teaspoons) butter or margarine, melted

125 g (4 oz) sliced ham

125 g (4 oz) mushrooms, sliced

6 tablespoons crushed, sieved tomatoes

125 g (4 oz/1 cup) grated Cheddar cheese

salt and pepper

watercress sprigs, to garnish

Preheat oven to 220C (425F/Gas 7). Spread dough with the French mustard, if using, or brush with the melted butter or margarine.

Slice the ham diagonally to form diamond shapes. Arrange over dough. Place one-third of the mushrooms in the centre and the remainder in groups around the edge of the pizza. Spoon a little tomato over mushrooms. Sprinkle with grated cheese. Season to taste with salt and pepper and bake in the oven for 20 minutes until dough is crisp and golden and the cheese bubbling. Garnish with watercress.

Serves 6.

SAUSAGE & ONION PIZZA

1 quantity Traditional Pizza Dough, shaped and ready for topping, see pages 10 and 11

TOPPING:

500 g (1 lb) pork chipolata sausages

30 g (1 oz/6 teaspoons) butter or margarine

1 large onion, finely sliced

125 g (4 oz) mushrooms, quartered

4 tablespoons sieved tomatoes

celery leaves, to garnish

Preheat oven to 220C (425F/Gas 7). Make topping. Heat grill on high. Cook sausages. Meanwhile, melt butter in a saucepan and cook onion gently until soft. Add mushrooms and tomatoes and cook, stirring, for 5 minutes. Drain sausages on absorbent kitchen paper. Slice diagonally.

Spoon the onion mixture over dough and top with sausage slices. Bake in the oven for 20 minutes until dough is crisp and golden. Serve garnished with celery leaves.

Serves 6.

MUSHROOM CALZONI

1 quantity Traditional Pizza Dough, made to end of step 2, see pages 10 and 11

1 tablespoon olive oil

beaten egg, to glaze

grated Parmesan cheese and oregano sprigs, to garnish

FILLING:

500 g (1 lb) open mushrooms, sliced

2 tablespoons olive oil

1 clove garlic, sliced

salt and pepper

½ teaspoon dried oregano

250 g (8 oz) ricotta or curd cheese

2 tablespoons freshly grated Parmesan cheese

Make the filling. In a saucepan, cook mushrooms in oil with garlic for 3-4 minutes. Remove with a slotted spoon and place in a bowl. Season to taste with salt and pepper; add oregano. Mix in ricotta or curd cheese and Parmesan.

Preheat oven to 220C (425F/ Gas 7). Grease 2 baking sheets. Divide dough into 2 equal pieces. Roll out both pieces on a lightly floured surface to circles measuring 25 cm (10 in) in diameter. Brush lightly with oil.

Divide filling between the 2 pieces of dough, confining it to one half of each circle. Dampen edges with water, then fold over dough to enclose filling and seal well by pressing with a fork. Transfer to baking sheets, brush with beaten egg and make 2 or 3 air holes with a sharp knife. Bake in the oven for 20 minutes until golden. Garnish with grated Parmesan cheese and sprigs of oregano.

Serves 4-6.

LEEK & ONION CALZONI

1 quantity Traditional Pizza dough, made up to end of step 2, see pages 10 and 11

1 tablespoon olive oil

beaten egg, to glaze

leek, onion and olive slices, to garnish

FILLING:

3 tablespoons olive oil

2 small leeks, sliced

2 onions, sliced

1 large Spanish onion, sliced

125 ml (4 fl oz/½ cup) dry white wine

125 ml (4 fl oz/½ cup) single (light) cream

salt and pepper

freshly grated nutmeg, to taste

125 g (4 oz) stuffed olives, chopped

Make filling. Heat oil and cook leeks and onions gently for 10 minutes until soft. Increase heat, add wine and cook until almost dry.

Reduce heat, add cream and season to taste with salt, pepper and nutmeg. Cook for 2-3 minutes until creamy. Remove from heat, stir in olives and set aside.

Preheat oven to 220C (425F/Gas 7). Grease 2 baking sheets. Divide dough into 2 equal pieces. Roll out both pieces on a lightly floured surface to circles measuring 25 cm (10 in) in diameter. Brush lightly with oil.

Divide filling between the 2 pieces of dough, confining it to one half of each circle. Dampen edges with water, then fold over dough to enclose filling and seal well by pressing with a fork. Transfer to baking sheets, brush with beaten egg and make 2 or 3 air holes with a sharp knife. Bake in the oven for 20 minutes until golden. Serve garnished with leek, onion and olive slices.

Serves 4-6.

BROCCOLI CALZONI

1 quantity Deep Pan Pizza Dough, made up to end of step 1, see page 14
1 teaspoon dried dill weed
1 tablespoon olive oil
beaten egg, to glaze
chopped fresh dill, to garnish
FILLING:
375 g (12 oz) broccoli
250 g (8 oz/2 cups) grated Cheddar cheese
salt and pepper

In a saucepan of boiling water, blanch broccoli for 2 minutes. Drain and refresh with cold water. Drain again. Chop coarsely.

Preheat oven to 220C (425F/Gas 7). Grease 2 baking sheets. Knead dough with dill weed until evenly distributed. Divide into 2 equal pieces. Roll out each piece on a lightly floured surface to a circle measuring 25 cm (10 in) in diameter. Brush lightly with oil.

Divide broccoli between the 2 pieces of dough, confining it to one half of each circle. Sprinkle with two-thirds of the cheese and season with salt and pepper. Dampen edges with water, fold over dough to enclose filling and seal well by pressing with a fork. Transfer to baking sheets, brush with beaten egg and sprinkle with remaining cheese. Make 2 or 3 air holes with a sharp knife. Bake in the oven for 20 minutes until golden. Serve the calzoni garnished with a little chopped fresh dill.

Serves 4-6.

LEAFY GREEN CALZONI

1 quantity Traditional Pizza Dough, made up to end of step 2, see pages 10 and 11

beaten egg, to glaze

tomato slices and marjoram sprigs, to garnish

FILLING:

500 g (1 lb) cabbage or spring greens

3 tablespoons olive oil

2 onions, chopped

440 g (14 oz) can tomatoes, drained

2 cloves garlic, crushed

½ teaspoon dried oregano

salt and pepper

Trim and discard hard stalks from cabbage or spring greens. Wash well and cook in a large saucepan (with just the water that clings to the leaves) for 10-15 minutes until tender. Drain well and chop finely.

Heat 2 tablespoons oil in a saucepan; cook onions until soft. Chop tomatoes, add to pan with garlic and oregano and salt and pepper to taste.

Cook for 20 minutes until thick.

Preheat oven to 220C (425F/Gas 7). Grease 2 baking sheets. Knock back risen dough and knead briefly. Divide dough into 2 equal pieces. Roll out both pieces on a lightly floured surface to circles measuring 25 cm (10 in) in diameter. Lightly brush with remaining oil.

Mix tomato mixture with the cooked greens. Divide between the 2 pieces of dough, confining mixture to one half of each circle. Dampen edges with water. Fold dough over to cover filling and seal well by pressing with a fork. Place on baking sheets, brush with beaten egg and make 2 or 3 air holes with a sharp knife. Bake for 20 minutes until golden. Cut in half. Serve hot, garnished with tomato and marjoram.

Serves 4.

COUNTRY CALZONI

| 1 quantity Traditional Pizza Dough, made up to end of step 2, see pages 10 and 11 |
| 2 tablespoons olive oil |
| mushroom slices and thyme sprigs, to garnish |
| FILLING: |
| 4 large pork sausages with herbs |
| 315 g (10 oz) goat's cheese, such as Chèvre |
| 6-8 dried tomatoes in oil, see Note |
| 125 g (4 oz) mushrooms, sliced |
| 2 dried red chillies, crushed |
| beaten egg, to glaze |

Preheat oven to 220C (425F/Gas 7). Grease 2 baking sheets. Knock back risen dough and knead briefly. Divide dough into 2 equal pieces. Roll both out on a lightly floured surface to circles measuring 25 cm (10 in) in diameter. Brush lightly with oil.

Remove skin from sausages and discard. Break sausagemeat into small pieces and sprinkle over both circles of dough, confining it to one half of circle. Chop cheese roughly and sprinkle over sausagemeat. Cut dried tomatoes into pieces and sprinkle over with mushrooms and crushed chillies.

Fold over dough to enclose filling, dampen edges with water and seal well by pressing with a fork. Transfer to baking sheets, brush with beaten egg and make 2 or 3 air holes with a sharp knife. Bake in the oven for 20 minutes until golden. Serve garnished with mushrooms and thyme.

Serves 4.

Note: Dried tomatoes in oil are available from Italian food shops and delicatessens.

INDEX